PEOPLE AT WORK

IN A CHILDREN'S HOSPITAL

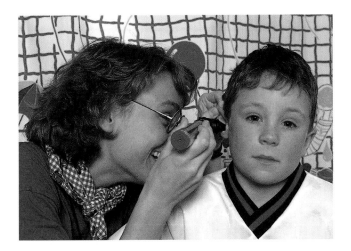

DEBORAH FOX

Evans

EVANS BROTHERS LIMITED

Published by Evans Brothers Limited
2a Portman Mansions
Chiltern Street
London
W1M 1LE

© 2000 Evans Brothers Limited

First published in 2000

Commissioned by: Su Swallow
Design: Neil Sayer
Photography: Alan Towse
Illustrator: Liam Bonney/The Art Market

British Library Cataloguing in Publication Data

Fox, Deborah
  People at work in a hospital
  1.Medical personnel - Juvenile literature 2. Hospitals -
  Juvenile literature
  I.Title II.In a hospital
  610.6'9

ISBN 0237519631

Printed in Hong Kong by Wing King Tong

Acknowledgements

The author and publisher wish to thank the staff and patients
at the Manchester Royal Children's Hospital and Aaron McGill
and his parents for their kind co-operation.

Contents

On the ward

I'm Andy and I am a nurse in a children's hospital. I work on the orthopaedic ward where we look after children who have broken bones and need surgery, or children who have other problems with their bones. Today I am in charge on the ward as I am the most senior nurse here.

New patients

▲ Andy and Aaron.

▼ Part of the nursing team on the orthopaedic ward.

When a new patient arrives on the ward, one of the nurses writes down the child's personal details on a 'new admission' form. We have to keep records of all patients on the ward. All the patients have had surgery or are about to have surgery. Some children can be here for up to ten weeks, and some may need to come in again for another operation. One of our patients, Aaron, came here about four months ago when he had an operation to straighten his foot. He is going back to the operating theatre this morning to have the frame on his leg removed.

▶ The doctor gives Aaron a check-up before the operation. After the operation, the doctor will check on him again.

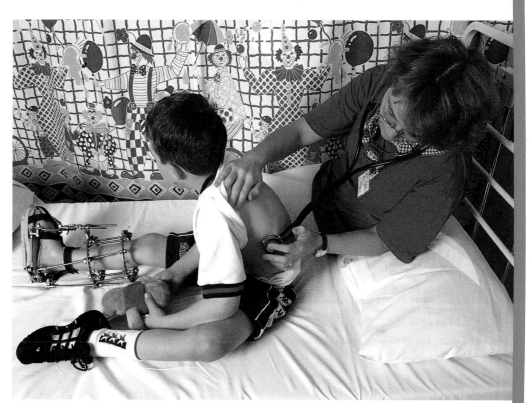

▼ The anaesthetist talks to Aaron about the operation and explains how he will send him to sleep.

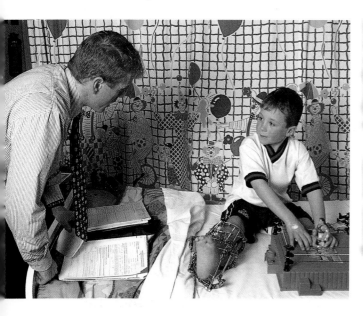

When children are in the ward for a long time, close relationships are built up between the child, the family and the nurse. Gaining the trust and friendship of children who are poorly and then helping them to get better and enjoy being in the hospital is wonderful.

Doctors

A doctor comes to the ward to give patients a check-up before they go to the operating theatre. The doctor explains to the children and their parents what sort of medicines they will have after the operation to relieve pain. Another doctor, an anaesthetist, visits the patients too. Anaesthetists make sure the child is unconscious throughout the operation and they check the child's breathing and heartbeat.

Going to theatre

All operations take place in an operating theatre, which is a set of three rooms – the anaesthetic room, the theatre and the recovery room. Teams of people are specially trained to work in theatres. Each day there is a list of patients who will be operated on, but, if there is an emergency case, the theatre team will deal with it straight away.

Operations go on every day of the year, all day and all night if necessary.

▼ *The theatre porter takes patients to and from theatre. I check the paperwork with the operating department practitioner.*

The theatre team

If children can't walk up to theatre, then theatre porters take them on a trolley. When Aaron arrives in theatre, an operating department practitioner, who assists the anaesthetist, prepares

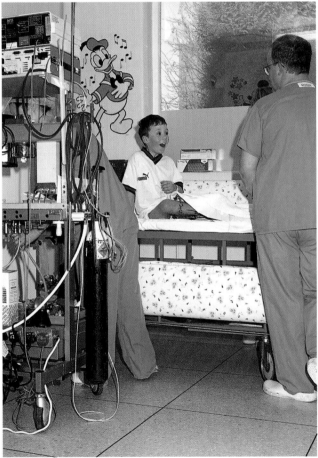

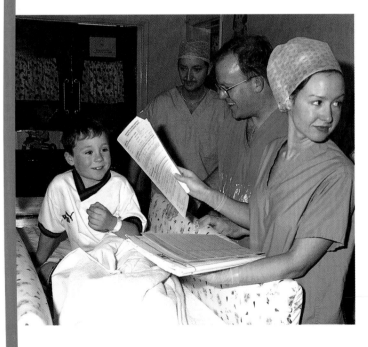

▲ *I talk to Aaron in the anaesthetic room. It's nice to share a joke with the patients before surgery.*

Aaron for the anaesthetic that will send him to sleep.

There are always at least four people for each operation, and often more. The surgeon operates on the patient and the surgeon's assistant, a nurse, makes sure the surgeon has all the correct instruments to perform the operation and that the operating theatre is completely sterile, or clean. Sometimes there is an auxiliary nurse too, who will help the nurse.

Scrubbing up

Before an operation all members of the team clean or 'scrub' their hands and arms with an antiseptic soap to make sure they are thoroughly sterile. After scrubbing up they put on their masks, gowns and gloves. They cannot touch anything until they are in theatre. If they do, they must scrub up again.

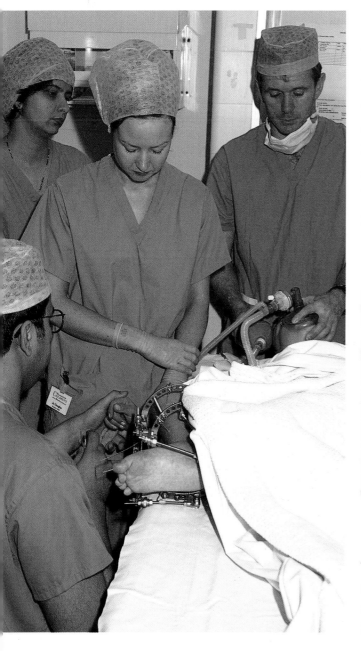

I became an anaesthetist because I had tried lots of different areas in medicine and I liked anaesthetics the most. It's a challenging job, but at times stressful and sad. I'm sad when I see very sick children in intensive care. That's difficult.

Dr Adam Dobson, anaesthetist

◀ The anaesthetist gives Aaron gas and air to send him to sleep just before the operation. A member of his team checks that Aaron is fully unconscious.

In theatre

Aaron has worn the leg frame for fifteen weeks, ever since he had the operation to straighten his foot. The frame has been specially made to fit Aaron's leg. It is a simple procedure to remove the frame and takes the surgeon about ten minutes.

Putting the leg in plaster

I come back to theatre just as the frame is removed so that I am ready to plaster Aaron's leg. Learning how to plaster is an essential part of the orthopaedic nurse's job and learning the basics takes about two to three months. As new techniques and products are introduced, we learn

▼ *The surgeon uses pliers to cut the wires that hold the frame in place. As soon as the frame is removed, Aaron's leg is cleaned with antiseptic fluid.*

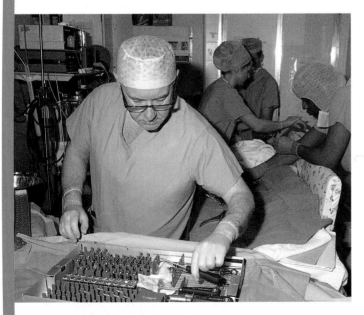

▲ *The surgeon, Mr John Day, selects the correct instrument for removing the leg frame.*

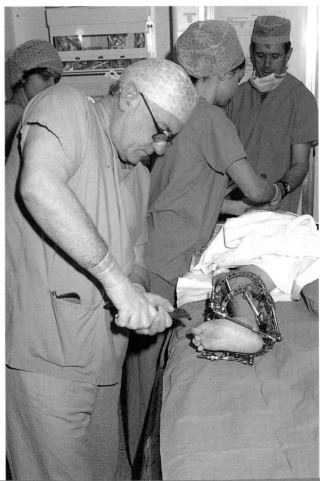

more. I must make sure that Aaron's ankle is plastered at a right angle, otherwise his foot will hurt once the plaster is removed and it may not move properly. I don't plaster his toes because the doctors check Aaron's blood circulation and his sense of feeling by testing his toes.

Recovery

As the anaesthetic begins to wear off, Aaron is taken to the recovery room, where he is looked after by a nurse and the operating department practitioner.

As soon as he is conscious, he is taken back to the ward to see his parents.

> I have worked in this hospital as a surgeon for over 20 years. If you get a case that is complex and works well, then it is very satisfying.
>
> John Day, consultant orthopaedic surgeon

▼ The plaster starts to set after two minutes and so I have to work quickly. It will be dry in one or two hours, but not completely set for two days. Only then is it possible to write on the plaster!

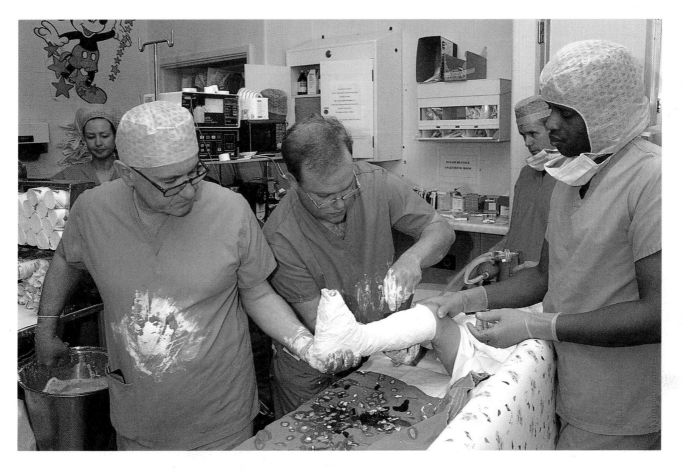

Accident and emergency

Accident and emergency covers everything from the stitching of cut fingers to major life-saving treatments. A&E is ideal for doctors who can think quickly. We work with a simple 'ABC' method for emergencies – checking the Airway first, then Breathing and then Circulation.

Dr Lorcan Duane, accident and emergency consultant

Some of our patients come from accident and emergency, which is sometimes known as A&E or casualty. Patients who have been involved in anything from a minor injury to a major accident come to this unit first.

Assessing patients

Patients report first of all to the receptionist, who types in their personal details on the computer. The patients are then seen by an A&E nurse, who assesses how urgent each case is. The unit uses a colour-coding system to put the patients in order of priority. It is a method of getting the right doctors to the right patients at the right time. If there is a serious case, then of course the patient would be seen immediately.

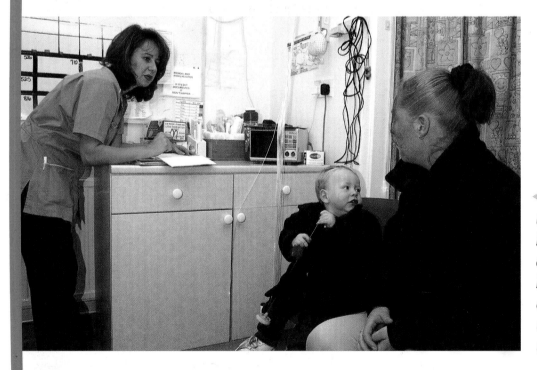

◀ Any patient who is under sixteen must be accompanied by an adult. This little boy's mother explains to the nurse what she thinks is wrong with her son.

The casualty doctor examines the little boy before sending him for an x-ray.

Nurses and their grades

Lead nurse/Senior Sister or Senior
 Charge Nurse (male) – top grade
Unit managers/Nurse specialist
Ward manager
Junior Sister/Junior Charge Nurse
Staff Nurse
Nursery Nurse
Auxiliary Nurse

The casualty doctor

Doctors who work in accident and emergency in this children's hospital also work at a general hospital for both adults and children. They work here to gain better knowledge of children's injuries, because about a third of the patients who go to accident and emergency departments in a general hospital are children. The doctor may send a child for further tests to other departments in the hospital or to a nurse in the unit for treatment.

Taking samples

Patients may need to give blood or urine samples to show if there are any signs of infection. Nurses check the samples. If they look abnormal, then the samples will be sent to the laboratories for more detailed tests.

▶ *Student nurses gain valuable experience working on different wards. This student nurse tests a urine sample from one of the patients, matching it against a colour guide.*

Looking inside the body

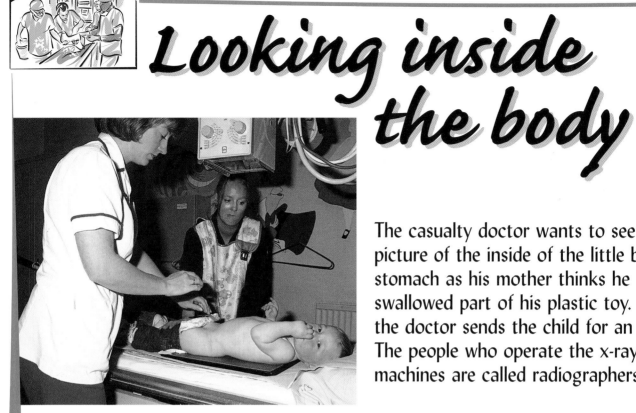

▲ The radiographer has positioned the x-ray machine over the child's stomach.

▼ The film from the x-ray is produced a few minutes later. The radiographer returns it to the casualty doctor who explains the results to the little boy's mother.

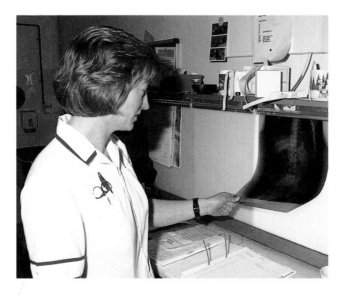

The casualty doctor wants to see a picture of the inside of the little boy's stomach as his mother thinks he has swallowed part of his plastic toy. So the doctor sends the child for an x-ray. The people who operate the x-ray machines are called radiographers.

MRI scanning

Radiographers can use different methods to look inside the human body. Taking an x-ray is the best method for showing up hard substances inside the body, such as bone or something someone may have swallowed, like a coin.

But doctors also need to see the soft parts of the human body, parts like the brain and the heart. They use a different machine to take pictures of the soft parts and this machine is called a 'magnetic resonance imaging scanner', or MRI scanner for short.

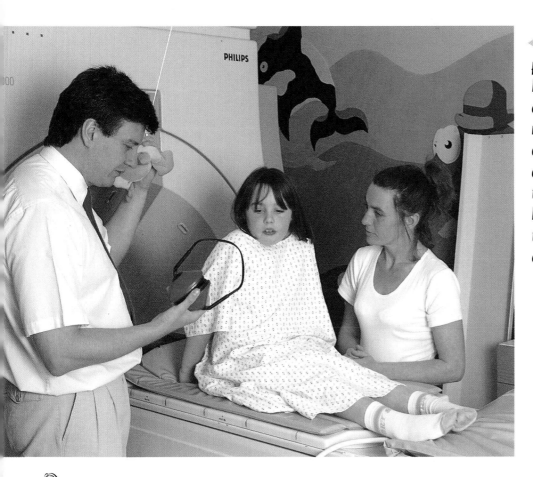

The radiographer prepares the patient, Emma, for the scan of her spine and the muscles inside it. He explains to Emma and her mother that the machine is very loud and so wearing the earphones will cut out the noise.

MRI scanning

- A scan of the spine takes about 30 minutes. The radiographers take 6 pictures and each picture takes about 5 minutes. If the patient moves at all, then the picture has to be retaken.
- An MRI scanning machine costs approximately £700,000.
- Radiographers sometimes inject dyes to show up specific organs.
- Nothing magnetic is allowed in the scanning room because metal is attracted to the machine.

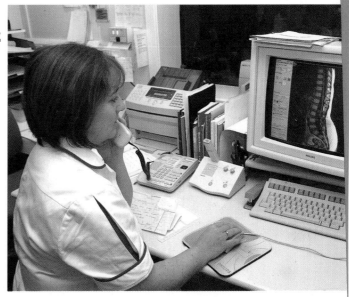

Another radiographer checks that Emma is keeping quite still. She can see the pictures of Emma's spine on her computer screen.

Finding out what's wrong

I chose radiology because I like seeing what is going on inside the body. I can find out what is wrong with a patient by looking at the pictures we take. I record a cassette tape of what I find and my report is then typed up by the secretary and sent back to the doctor. If I find something that needs urgent attention, then I will call the doctor immediately.

Dr Neville Wright,
consultant radiologist

Doctors who find out, or diagnose, what is wrong with patients by looking at x-rays and scans, such as MRI scans, are called radiologists. All doctors study for a degree in medicine and then spend a few years in a hospital getting general experience. After that they specialise in a branch of medicine, such as radiology or surgery.

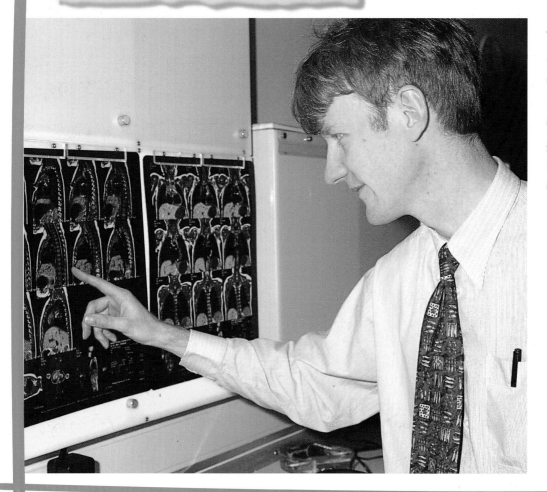

The radiologist studies the film from an MRI scan. He can see from the scans any problems the patient may have with blood vessels around the heart.

18

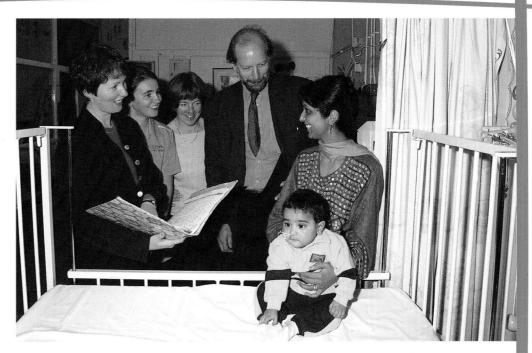

▶ The consultant paediatricians (children's doctors), a staff nurse and a dietician go on regular ward rounds to see all the patients.

Ward rounds

The ward round is an excellent way for the doctors, nurses and health-care workers to talk to patients. Normally the team meets first to discuss complex cases and test results, such as a blood test result or a radiologist's report. Ward rounds can take from one to three hours, depending on the number of patients and how ill they are. When medical students go on the ward round, doctors ask them questions about diagnosing illnesses and treatments. This is part of their training.

I enjoy looking after children. They are much more honest and open than adults. I trained as an adult nurse and then did my children's nursing course. All the children on my ward have got cancer. Many of them need strong drugs that can make them sick or lose their hair. Seeing them smile and laugh makes our job as nurses worthwhile.

Chris, ward manager

Doctors and their grades

House officer (HO) – after Medical School, doctors spend a year gaining general experience in an adult hospital

Senior House officer (SHO) – a junior qualified doctor

Specialist Registrar – a middle-grade qualified doctor

Consultant – the senior level; the average age for a first position as a consultant is 32

In the laboratories

The people who work in the medical laboratories are called biomedical scientists. They help to diagnose what is wrong with patients by examining fluids from their bodies, such as blood, saliva and urine. They also find out what germs are in infected parts of the body. By studying the germs, they can discover the best way of killing them.

Analysing samples

When a sample comes in to the biomedical laboratory, it is recorded in the log book and given a bar code. Doctors send a 'request card' with the sample asking the scientists to do certain tests. High-tech equipment now does a lot of the work biomedical scientists used to do. The laboratory staff load blood samples, for example, into a machine that separates the blood into parts that can be analysed. Another machine analyses the blood and gives the results to a computer.

▲ *The nurse hands in some samples to the biomedical laboratory.*

▶ *The biomedical scientist puts 'cuvettes' containing blood samples into trays. Then she will load them into the analysing machine.*

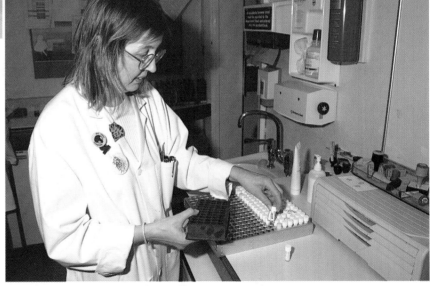

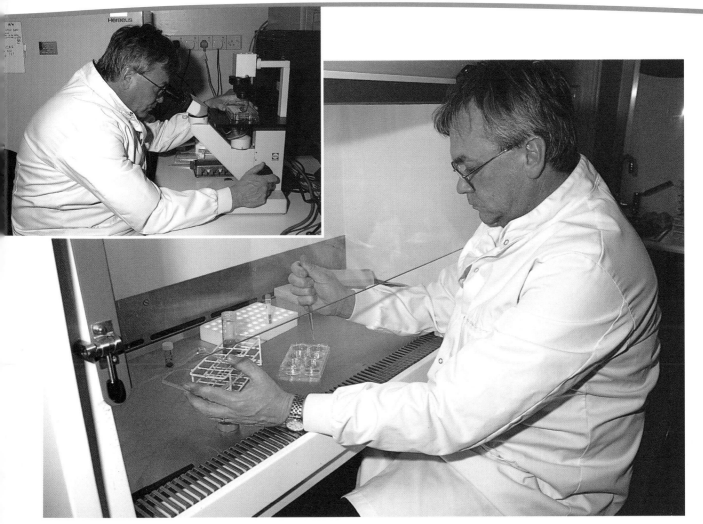

▲ This scientist analyses a patient's bone marrow.

Bone marrow

Bone marrow is a vital part of our bodies as it is where blood is made. Some rare diseases can kill a person's bone marrow and sometimes the treatment for other diseases can kill it too. So doctors take the bone marrow out of the patient's body and store it until the patient gets better. If the bone marrow is already diseased and cannot be cured, then another person's bone marrow can be put, or transplanted, into the patient's body.

I have worked at this hospital since bone marrow transplants were first introduced 11 years ago. When I arrived here, we didn't have the techniques to do a lot of the things we can do now.

A few weeks ago, we had a party for all the transplant patients. When I saw a patient who had gone through a transplant ten years ago and who is now expecting a baby, it gave me a tremendous boost.

Trevor, clinical scientist

Medicines and diet

Some medicines control pain and some help cure illnesses. All the medicines in hospital come from the pharmacy department. The department is divided into two main areas, one where they prepare 'ready-made' medicines for the wards and patients, and another where they prepare medicines that must be kept completely free from germs.

Some children must have medicines that are specially made up for them. There is a separate area in the pharmacy for doing this.

Dispensary

Pharmacy technicians regularly visit all the wards to re-stock their medicines. They also 'dispense', or give out, medicines to patients who are about to leave hospital or who are in just for the day. A pharmacist always checks and signs out the medicines before they leave the dispensary.

▼ A *pharmacy technician dispenses medicines for the outpatients' department.*

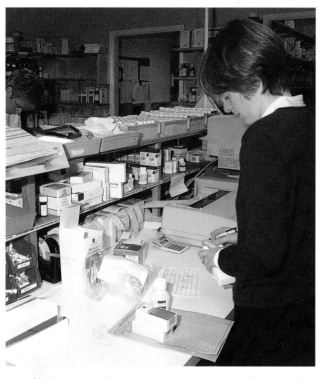

▲ A *pharmacist prepares some medicines for one of the wards.*

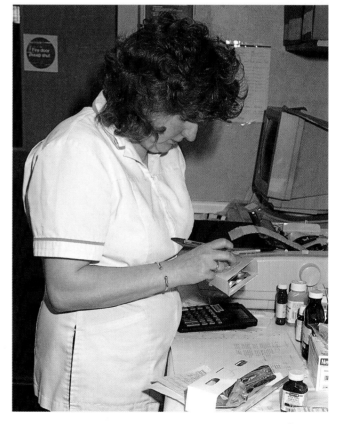

The aseptic suite

Some medicines, such as antibiotic injections, have to be prepared in the aseptic suite, which is a sterile area. Here pharmacy technicians also prepare the bags of liquid food that are fed directly into some patients' stomachs. Everyone wears a sterile gown, a hat, shoes and gloves. The pharmacists and technicians take turns to work in the aseptic suite and the dispensary to keep their skills up to date.

▼ *The dietician has a bottle of liquid food for Peter, who has been getting treatment for a tumour. He has been having liquid food for a year to give him extra nutrition and to help build up his weight.*

Food and nutrition

When people are ill, they must keep strong by eating the correct diet. Dieticians work with doctors and nurses to plan what sort of food patients should be eating. In this hospital, the dieticians deal with a wide range of problems and illnesses, such as underweight and overweight children, diabetic children and those suffering from cancer.

Sometimes children are too ill to eat as much as they need, or too ill to eat at all, but they still need all the essential nutrients that food provides. So, instead, they have liquid food that is fed directly into their stomachs.

Home life in hospital

Children who are in hospital miss their home and their family. Going to hospital can be frightening. All the people who work in the hospital understand how hard it can be and they try to make it a friendly and welcoming place. Family-care officers can arrange for a member of each patient's family to stay at the hospital, even if it means having a camp bed in one of the play rooms.

Keeping up with schoolwork

Children who are in hospital don't miss out on their education. The hospital has two schools with 32 teachers and 13 nursery teachers who look after toddlers. Some lessons are held in computer rooms in some of the wards. The teachers talk to the children's school to find out what stage they are up to in each subject.

▶ *This teacher helps a pupil with his French GCSE language work.*

As a teacher in a hospital, I have to get used to people interrupting classes. Nurses may want a blood sample, or a child may need to go to physiotherapy. I have to be flexible and prepared to work in different places. I work in the hospital school, on the wards and in a child's home too.

Liz, teacher

Mealtimes

Over 40 people work in the hospital kitchens and restaurants, preparing food for patients and staff. At the beginning of the week, the catering staff send menus to the wards so that

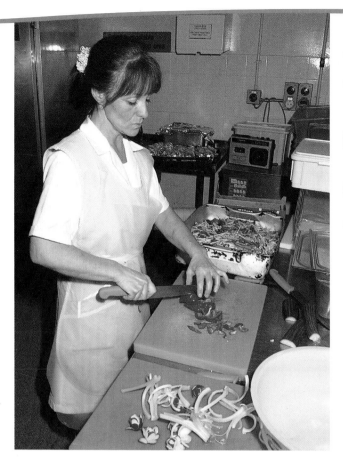

Hospital food used to have a bad reputation. We try to give the children the food they want, so we've got steak pie, hot dogs, turkey burgers and chips on our menus. Today we're having a party buffet with dinosaur-shaped crispy bites, crisps and sandwiches.

Vanessa, Deputy Catering Manager

◁ Some food, such as this stir-fry, is cooked in the hospital; the rest is bought in ready prepared.

▽ This play specialist uses fibre-optic lights to stimulate the baby's eyesight, which has been weakened because of a rare illness.

children can choose what they want to eat. The children and their parents also fill in questionnaires on what other food they'd like to have. Dieticians talk to the catering staff to work out individual menus for children who need a special diet.

Playing in hospital

The hospitals recognise how important it is for children to play. The wards are brightly decorated and each one has a play room, televisions and computers. Play therapists use role play to help children understand new experiences like having an x-ray or an MRI scan.

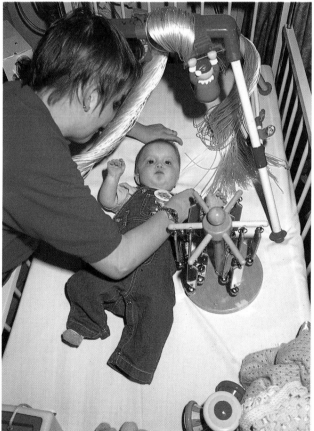

To outpatients'

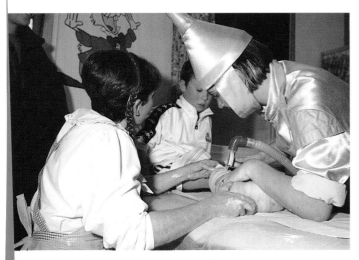

▲ The plaster saw is loud. It sounds like a dentist's drill. Because it's nearly Christmas, the nurses are wearing fancy dress!

▼ The sister in the outpatients' department prises apart the plaster to free Aaron's leg.

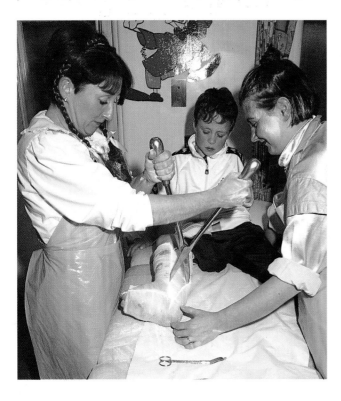

Six weeks have passed since I plastered Aaron's leg. It's time for the plaster to come off, so Aaron has come to the outpatients' department for the afternoon. As it is nearly Christmas, we like to get into the spirit of the season and dress up! The two nurses who are going to remove Aaron's plaster are dressed as Dorothy and the Tinman from *The Wizard of Oz*.

Freeing Aaron's leg

The staff nurse uses a saw to cut through the plaster because it is so strong. It takes about 20 minutes to do this. The sister then pushes apart the plaster. Once Aaron's leg is free, the nurses clean it and then a doctor examines it.

Making a splint

Aaron's leg hasn't healed properly yet. He needs to wear a 'splint' for another five or six months. The splint will support his leg until it heals properly. An orthotist needs to make a model of Aaron's leg so that the splint will fit. To make the model, he wraps some material called 'stockingnet' around

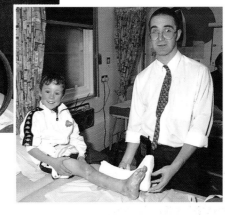

The orthotist wraps 'stockingnet' around Aaron's leg and sticks a blue plastic tube to it.

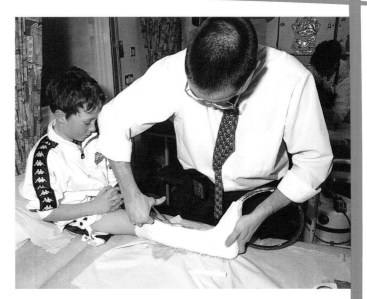

When the orthotist cuts the plaster, he uses the blue plastic as his cutting guide.

The orthotist now has a model of Aaron's leg. A splint will be made using this model.

Aaron's leg, which stops plaster sticking to it. Then he plasters the leg. When the plaster has dried, he cuts it off. He sends off this model and his instructions for making up the splint.

I thought the saw was going to cut me, but it only tickled and vibrated. Mr Day checked my leg to see if I needed another frame. I was pleased when he said I didn't! My foot feels much better now that the plaster has been taken off.

Aaron, a patient

This young boy's knee keeps dislocating. He exercises it in the pool, watched by his physiotherapist. Aaron, too, will go to see a physiotherapist to strengthen his foot.

Glossary

airway passage-way from mouth and nose to the lungs

anaesthetist a doctor who puts patients to sleep during operations and monitors their breathing, heartbeat and recovery after the operation

antibiotic special medicine that kills infection

cancer a disease that can produce uncontrolled swellings or blood problems

check-up an examination by a doctor or a nurse

degree a course of study at university; students take a degree in medicine for five years or a degree in nursing for a minimum of three years

diabetic a person who has an illness that prevents his or her body from controlling the amount of sugar in the blood

dislocating when a bone is knocked out of position from its joint

medicine the science of diagnosing, preventing and curing disease

nutrients the substances in food that keep a person healthy

operating theatre the place where the surgeon operates

orthopaedics the branch of surgery concerned with correcting problems of the bones and joints

pharmacy the department that makes up and gives out drugs (medicines)

physiotherapy the use of exercise, massage and movement to help people re-gain mobility

radiology the study of x-rays and scans

saliva the fluid in the mouth that helps the digestion of food

splint a support for an injured part of the body, usually a fractured bone; a splint is rigid and supports the broken bone so that it can rest and heal together

surgery the branch of medicine concerned with treating injuries or diseases and performing operations

Index

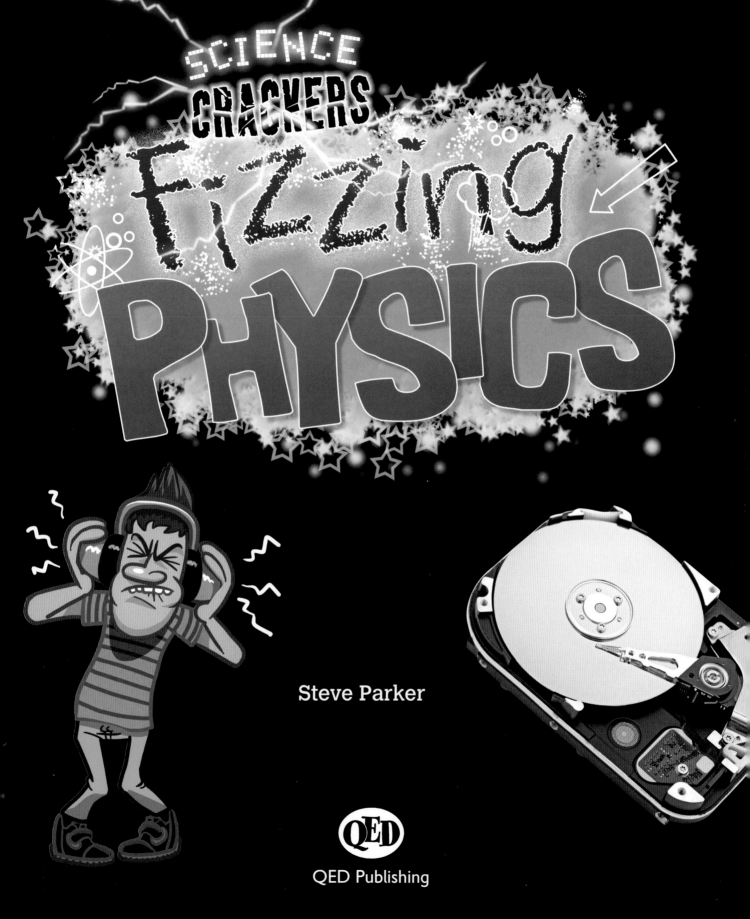

SCIENCE CRACKERS

Fizzing PHYSICS

Steve Parker

QED

QED Publishing

Created for QED Publishing by Tall Tree Ltd
www.talltreebooks.co.uk
Editors: Rob Colson and Jennifer Sanderson
Designers: Jonathan Vipond and Malcolm Parchment
Illustrations, activities: Lauren Taylor
Illustrations, cartoons: Bill Greenhead

First published in the UK in 2011 by
QED Publishing
A Quarto Group company
226 City Road
London EC1V 2TT

www.qed-publishing.co.uk

A catalogue record for this book is available from the British Library.

ISBN 978 1 84835 558 3

Printed in China

Picture credits
(t=top, b=bottom, l=left, r=right, c=centre, fc=front cover)
Alamy: 17c Myrleen Pearson; **Corbis** 12b New Sport, 26br Gavin Hellier/Robert Harding World Images; **Creative Commons** 17t and 31 Brian Gratwicke, 18tr Rob Shenk; **Dreamstime** 18bl Elena Elisseeva, 19cl Kiselev Adriy Valerevich,; **istockphoto** 23br Embosser; **Shutterstock** 1 and 27t Ragnarock, 2 and 6t Regien Paassen, 4bc Gluestock, 4bl Elisanth, 4tr Sergey Lavrenter, 5t Andrew Horwitz, 5c Rena Schild, 4br Rynio Productions, 6b Brett Mulcany, 7b Gilmanshin, 7 Greg Epperson, 9c Robert Spriggs, 9b Chen Wei Seng, 10b Matt Jones, 10–11 Sergey Utkin, 11tr Yuriy Zhuravov, 11b and 23 tr Daniel Gale, 12t Scott O Smith, 13l Eric J Enger, 13tr Sascha Gebhardt, 14l Antony McAulay, 14r daphne, 15t vlue, 15bl hj schneider, 16b Ferenc Szelepcsenyi, 16t Adisa, 19cr Olaf Speier, 19b Sergei Butorin, 22 Kevan O'Meara, 23bl Olga Besnard, 23 bl Vitezslav Halamka, 23cr Gordana, 23br Tatiana Popova, 23 cr ps-42, 25bl valzan, 25bc loriklaszio, 25 br gresei, 26t Awe Inspiring Images, 27b Vibrant Image Studio, 27b dubassy, 28c 13848535, 28r Yuri Arcurs, 28b Filatov Alexey, **SPL** 17r Andrew Lambert Photography, 19tr Joe McDonald/Visuals Unlimited, 28 Alex Bartel

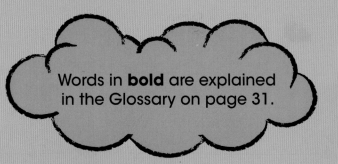

Words in **bold** are explained in the Glossary on page 31.

CONTENTS

MACHINES EVERYWHERE

It is a hot day and you need an ice-cold drink. You have a bottle of fruit juice, but its metal top is fixed on very hard. Using a bottle opener, you lever it off.

A bottle opener is a type of machine, called a lever. It lets you move something using a big **force**, but only a small way. Another simple machine is the wheel. You can roll a heavy load on it without too much effort. Ramps or steps are also simple machines. They let you move something upwards in small, easy stages.

PLAY MACHINES

A playground has machines, not for work, but for fun. A see-saw is a lever and a roundabout is a type of wheel. There may be a pulley on a rope, too.

Simple machines

The main simple machines are ramps, wedges (such as an axe blade), wheels and axles, screws (right), pulleys, gears and levers. A ring-pull on a drinks can (left) is a lever. You can combine these simple machines to make more complicated ones. For example, a wheelbarrow (above) has levers for handles as well as a wheel.

MENDING MACHINES

When your bicycle breaks, you might use a simple machine to mend it. To tighten a nut, you need a spanner. This is a type of lever. It moves a nut a small distance, but with a great deal of force.

IMAGINE THIS...

Machines make jobs easier! Imagine what your life would be like if you did not have machines to help you.

WHEELS

The wheel is the ideal machine for rolling things along. You do not have to lift anything, you just push or pull. You can also use wheels on bicycles to zoom along quickly and easily.

5

GO AND STOP

IMAGINE THIS...
If something moves fast then suddenly stops, it can be damaged or harmed. This is why people wear seat belts in cars.

Many machines, from cars to jumbo jets, give you the force to keep moving. Their force comes from engines, but there are also natural forces that can move us, such as **gravity**.

Some forces, such as friction, or rubbing make us slow down and stop. You can feel friction when you rub your finger against a rough surface – your finger will not slide easily over the rough surface. Friction can make things difficult to move. But it can be very helpful at keeping us in one place and in slowing us down.

FORCE OF GRAVITY
One force that works everywhere on the Earth is gravity. It pulls things downwards. On a downwards slope, such as a roller-coaster track, gravity makes the roller-coaster speed up.

SHOWING MOVEMENT

At an air display, the smoke trails from planes show how they move. They climb, turn and go up and over and down in a circle, a move called looping the loop.

LIFE-SAVING FRICTION

Without friction, climbers would fall off steep rocks. Climbers test each hand grip or foot hold to make sure there is enough friction so that they can cling on.

USEFUL FRICTION

Most of a motorcycle's working parts are smooth, hard and well-oiled. But not the brakes! They press on the wheel brake disc to cause friction and make the motorcycle slow down.

ON THE SLIDE

Friction is the force that stops your plate sliding off your meal tray. Try this to see for yourself how friction works.

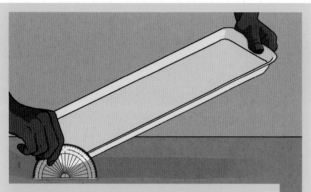

1 With the tray on a flat table, lift one end slightly. Practise measuring its angle with the protractor. A friend can help by looking at the angle from the front.

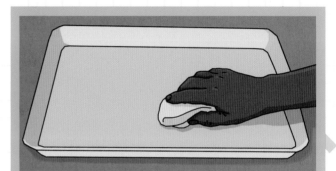

3 Put some cooking oil on some kitchen towel and smear the tray with the oil. Repeat step 2. The objects that stay on the tray at the highest angle have the most friction.

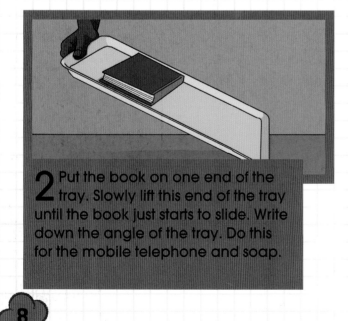

2 Put the book on one end of the tray. Slowly lift this end of the tray until the book just starts to slide. Write down the angle of the tray. Do this for the mobile telephone and soap.

4 Clean the tray. Put the marbles on it. Balance the book on the marbles. How does this change the angle at which the book starts to slide? Are the marbles more effective than the oil at reducing friction?

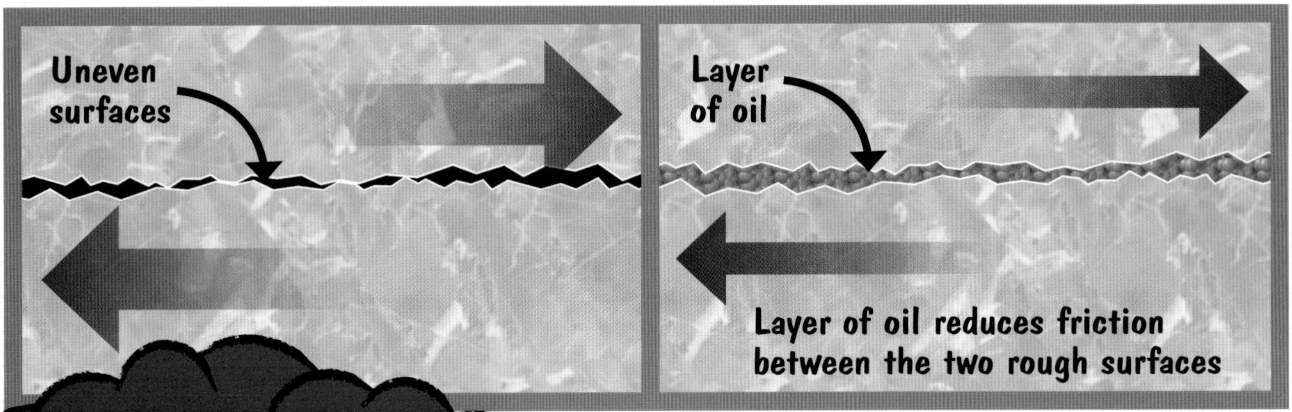

Uneven
surfaces

Layer
of oil

Layer of oil reduces friction
between the two rough surfaces

Every surface, even the smoothest, has tiny bumps and pits. The bigger these are, the more they rub and scrape past each other, and the greater the friction. Adding oil reduces the amount these bumps and pits rub together, and this lessens the friction.

SMOOTH RIDE

Objects roll more easily than they slide. Placing small balls between surfaces reduces friction as the balls roll rather than slide. Inside many machines, such as the wheels of a racing car, metal balls, called bearings, are used to reduce friction and keep the machines working efficiently.

MUBADALA
ABU DHABI

Santander

ETIHAD

Santand

LIGHT AND DARK

Darkness can be scary, especially if you do not know what is around you. Light is much better. Your eyes can see the shades, colours and patterns that surround you.

Things that give out light are called light sources. For us on the Earth, the brightest light source is the Sun. Substances that let light rays go through them, such as glass, are called **transparent**. Substances that stop light passing through, such as wood, are called **opaque**. Light rays travel in straight lines and cannot curve around objects, so on the far side of an opaque object is a dark area known as shadow.

DAY AND NIGHT

Sunlight travels through space before it reaches us. As the Earth spins, the part of its surface facing the Sun has day, while the part facing away has night.

NEED FOR LIGHT

Many animals need bright light to see their surroundings. Tropical fish come from warm places where the Sun is usually bright and strong. They need a powerful light in their tank so that they feel at home.

10

SPOOKY SHADOWS

The dark shape behind an opaque object is called its shadow, or umbra. The shadow is the same shape as the object that is blocking the light. This can be great fun when putting on a shadow puppet show!

MAKING LIGHT

When the Sun sets and it gets dark, we can make our own light by flicking a light switch. Electricity flows through a light bulb, causing it to glow and give out light, turning darkness into light.

11

SEE THE LIGHT

You see light sources, such as an electric bulb, because they give out their own rays of light. These travel through the air and into our eyes. However, chairs, trees, people and books do not give out their own light. So how do people see them?

Objects that are not light sources bounce back, or reflect, light that hits them. This is how you see them – by the light they reflect. If there is no light source, these objects would have no light to reflect, so we would not be able to see them.

MIRROR IMAGE

When you look in a mirror, you are seeing a reflection, which is a flipped image of yourself. If you raise your right arm, it looks like your image is raising its left arm.

REAR VIEW

Mirrors help you to see behind you. Racing car drivers wear helmets and are strapped in, so they cannot look over their shoulders. They have to use their rear-view and side mirrors.

MOONSHINE

The Moon does not make its own light. You can see it because it reflects sunlight. As it goes round the Earth, the Moon appears to change shape as the amount of its sunlit part that we see on Earth changes.

IMAGINE THIS...

A flat, shiny surface produces a reflection. Curved or bent surfaces reflect the light rays in a different way, so the image is an odd shape – which can be funny.

STILL WATER

The surface of still water is like a smooth mirror that reflects light from the scene into our eyes.

13

COLOURS GALORE

Most people like rainbows, but where do they come from? Ordinary white light from the Sun, a lamp or a torch is made of a mixture of all the colours of the rainbow. These are called the spectrum. Follow these steps to see them.

As white light travels from one substance to another, such as from the air into a glass prism or a raindrop, it bends, or refracts. Each colour refracts by a slightly different amount, so the colours separate to form a spectrum.

1 Next time it is both sunny and raining, look for a rainbow. Rainbows are formed by raindrops scattering rays of light.

2 Look at a DVD's blank side near a bright lamp. Twist and turn the DVD until you see a spectrum. You can probably angle it to see more than one spectrum!

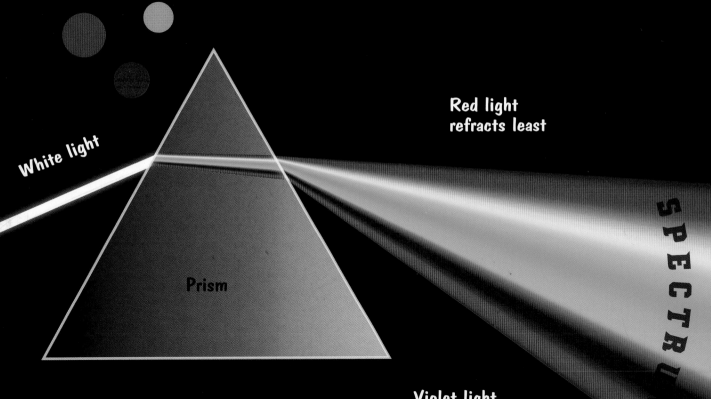

White light

Red light
refracts least

Prism

SPECTRUM

Violet light
refracts most

3 Next time you walk past a puddle, check it out for rainbow colours. They are usually caused by a thin layer of oil floating on the surface.

4 In a dark room, shine a torch through a clear glass of water onto some black card. Angle the beam of light to produce rainbow colours on the card.

STOP THAT NOISE!

People sometimes say: "It is so noisy, I can hardly hear myself think!" Loud noises can confuse people, while other sounds can be pleasant and relaxing.

Sounds travel through the air as sound waves. A sound comes from a source such as earphones, a television, an engine and your own voice. A sound source must shake to and fro quickly, known as **vibrating**, to make its waves.

Sounds that we like and enjoy can be made by musical instruments or birds or people singing. Noisy sounds, such as traffic or jet planes roaring past, dogs barking, vacuum cleaners and fire or burglar alarms are unpleasant. We usually want them to stop.

ANNOYING SOUNDS

Some sounds can be unpleasant. Loud, harsh sounds, such as noisy traffic, make us screw up our faces and put our hands over our ears to keep them out. After a while they put us in a bad mood.

MAKING MUSIC

Some sounds, such as those from the instruments in an orchestra, go well together. All kinds of objects can be used to make musical sounds, from hose pipes to rubbish bins!

ANIMAL SOUNDS

Animals use sounds to send messages. Dog barks can mean 'Beware!' A bird's song can be used to show off its lovely voice. Frog croaks and grasshopper chirps can often say 'Let's play!'

Frogs croak to attract mates

HUMAN SOUNDS

Everyone can be a sound source in a number of ways. You talk, shout and sing using the voicebox in your neck. You can use other body parts to make sounds. You can clap your hands and stamp your feet, and even whistle.

VIBRATE

Something must vibrate to produce a sound. This can be the vocal cords inside your voicebox or a string on a guitar. As it vibrates, it squeezes and stretches the air next to it, starting sound waves that move out.

IMAGINE THIS...

Male humpback whales sing long and beautiful songs to attract female humpbacks. Their songs can be heard by other whales hundreds of kilometres away.

17

FAST, HIGH AND LOUD

SOUNDS FAST!

Sound waves move through the air at about 340 metres per second. When jet fighters roar through the air faster than the speed of sound, they are called supersonic.

Sound waves travel through the air like waves travelling through a slinky (below), squashing and then stretching the air in turn.

The loudness of a sound is called its **volume**. If the radio is too quiet, you turn it up using the volume control. Whether a sound is high or low is called its **pitch**. This can range from the high cheep of a bird to the deep boom of thunder.

Wavelength

HIGH AND LOW

The pitch of a sound depends on the **wavelength** – this is the distance between each sound wave. The shorter the wavelength, the higher the sound.

Whisper 20dB

TOO HIGH FOR US

Noises that are too high-pitched for us to hear are called **ultrasound**. Bats find their way by making ultrasonic squeaks and listening to the echoes that bounce off objects.

Loud Shout 80-90dB

Chainsaw 100-110dB

Bomb expolding 200dB

QUIET AND LOUD

The loudness or volume of a sound is measured in decibels (dB).

19

BOTTLE PAN PIPES

You can make your own musical instruments from throw-away or recycled items around the house. Make your own pan pipes and blow your audience away with a good tune.

2 Put some water in one bottle and see how it changes the sound, making it higher in pitch. You may have to change how hard you blow.

1 Put the bottles in a row next to each other on a table. Blow across the top of one of them to make a hooting sound.

3 Put increasing amounts of water in the bottles along the row. In each bottle there is less air to shake, or vibrate, so the note is higher.

4 If you have a guitar or piano adjust the water to 'tune' the bottles. Now you are ready to play!

BUCKET DRUM

Once you've made the bottle pan pipes, you can build a drum kit and form your very own junkyard band.

YOU WILL NEED:

- empty tins and drinks cans of different sizes
- two large spoons
- old bucket (metal is best)
- sticky tape

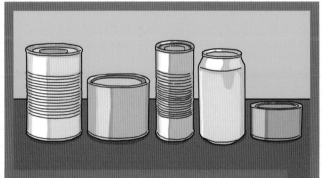

1 Tap each tin or can with a spoon to hear the pitch of the sound it makes. Put them in order from lowest to highest pitch.

3 Using your spoons as drumsticks, beat out the main rhythm on the bucket and add in faster taps on the tins and cans.

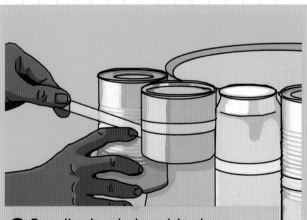

2 Turn the bucket upside-down. Tape the tins and cans in order around the bottom of the bucket, level with the bottom of the bucket.

You could make a 'guitar' with a shoebox and elastic bands. You could also tap a row of glass jars or bottles with different amounts of water in them to make a xylophone.

THAT'S ELECTRIC!

Electricity powers our modern world. It can be sent long distances along wires and it can be used in many ways, from lights to motors, heaters and sound equipment.

Only some substances carry electricity. They are known as electrical **conductors**. Most of these are metals. Copper and silver are especially good conductors. Water is also a good conductor. Substances that do not carry electricity are called electrical **insulators**. They include wood, plastic, card, fabrics and pottery or ceramics.

IMAGINE THIS...
Batteries might be handy and portable, but make sure that you use the right batteries for each appliance.

POWER STATIONS
Electricity is made in power stations. Some power stations burn fuel such as coal, oil or gas. This turns water into steam, which spins turbines to generate the electricity. Wind farms (above) use wind to spin turbines.

DANGER!

Wires, cables or power lines on big towers and pylons, and machinery such as transformers, all carry very strong electricity. You should never mess around with these, or with the plug sockets in your home.

HOW MUCH?

The strength of electricity is measured in volts (v). Voltages range from very low-powered batteries to very high levels in overhead power cables.

PORTABLE POWER

Batteries make electricity from chemicals. They power small moveable gadgets, such as toys, mobile telephones, music players and torches. They can also be used to power large devices, including cars, such as this Tesla Roadster. Instead of using petrol, you plug a battery-powered car in to recharge before zooming off again.

Tesla Roadster

HIGH

Grid
400,000 volts

Household mains
220-240 volts

Batteries
1.5-12 volts

LOW

POTATO POWER

Batteries make electricity from the combination of chemicals inside them. You can do the same using a potato!

YOU WILL NEED:

- two big fresh potatoes
- two short lengths of thick copper wire
- two **galvanized** nails
- two crocodile clips
- insulated wire
- light-emitting diode (LED)

1 Number the potatoes 1 and 2. Push a nail into each potato, most of the way down. Insert a piece of copper wire into each potato, as far away from the nail as possible.

2 Using the clips and insulated wire, connect the nail in potato 1 to the copper wire in potato 2.

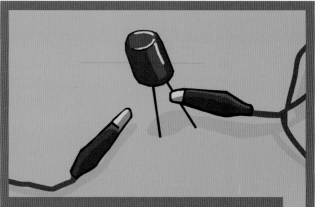

3 Again using the clips and insulated wire, connect the copper wire in potato 1 to one contact on the LED.

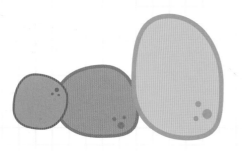

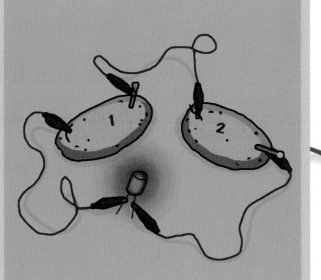

4 Finally connect the nail in potato 2 to the other contact on the LED. When you do this, you make a complete circuit, and electricity starts to flow. The electricity will make the LED glow.

Potatoes contain chemical energy. In the potato battery, the zinc on the galvanized nail, the chemicals in the potato and the copper in the thick wire, all react together to make an electric current.

Add more potatoes with their nails and copper wires to the circuit. Make sure you connect the nail of one to the copper wire of the next. Does the bulb glow brighter? Try fruits such as cucumbers, tomatoes, apples and bananas. Which one works best?

This device can measure the electric current of different objects — including fruit!

MYSTERY MAGNETS

One of the strangest forces cannot be seen, but can push or pull with huge power. This mysterious force is magnetism, and it is used in hundreds of machines.

Magnetism particularly affects iron objects. Steel is mostly iron, and is used to make many items, from cutlery to fridges. Magnets stick to these objects. A magnet has two poles where its force is strongest: one pole is North (N) and the other is South (S). When two magnets come close together, if their poles are 'like' or the same, they push apart, or repel. Two different or 'unlike' poles pull together, or attract.

FLOATING MAGNETS

Some trains use magnets to zoom along. A magnet underneath the train pushes against a magnet on the tracks with so much magnetic force that the train actually floats! This type of train is called a maglev train, which is short for 'magnetic levitation' (lifting).

MAGNETIC FIELD

The force of a magnet acts in an area called the magnetic field. The field curves around between the poles of the magnet. You can see this by scattering iron filings around a magnet. The iron filings will line up in the pattern of the magnetic field.

MAGNETS AND INFORMATION

Information is stored on computer hard discs as patterns of tiny magnetic spots. A hard disc is usually a stack of metal circles, each with a very thin magnetic coating.

IMAGINE THIS...

The main law of magnetism is like poles repel and unlike poles attract. So...

N + N = REPEL
S + S = REPEL
N + S = ATTRACT

FRIDGE MAGNETS

Small, button-shaped magnets with plastic covers can hold notes to a steel fridge casing. The magnetism passes through thin paper, but is much weaker with thicker paper or card.

USING MAGNETS

Some magnets have magnetism all the time. They are called permanent magnets. Others can be switched on and off because their magnetism comes from electricity. These are known as **electromagnets**.

As electricity flows along a wire, it makes a slight magnetic field around the wire. Usually, this is too weak to be useful. But if the wire is twisted into a coil, called a solenoid, then the magnetic force is made much stronger, turning it into an electromagnet. More electricity makes the magnet stronger and less electricity makes it weaker.

MOVED BY MAGNETS

Most car bodies are made of thin steel. At a scrapyard, cars are crushed to the size of a bed and lifted away by an electromagnet on a crane. Electromagnets are also used to sort steel and other iron-containing metals, from other substances so that they can be recycled.

MAGNETS IN MOTORS

Electric motors contain wire coils that spin around inside permanent magnets. The coils use electromagnetism to pull and push against the permanent magnets. This produces a turning force, which makes the motor spin.

Wire coil spins when electricity passes through it

MAGNETIC SOUNDS

Headphones make sounds when magnetism vibrates a tiny sheet inside them called the diaphragm. Louder sounds are produced when the magnetism is stronger and vibrates the diaphragm more.

IMAGINE THIS...

People rely on dozens of electric motors, from electric toothbrushes to washing machines, tumble dryers, vacuum cleaners and food blenders.

NAVIGATION

A compass is a magnetic needle that spins around to line up with the Earth's natural magnetic field, and points North and South.

29

MAGNETIC FISHING

You can discover which substances are magnetic and try your hand at fishing at the same time!

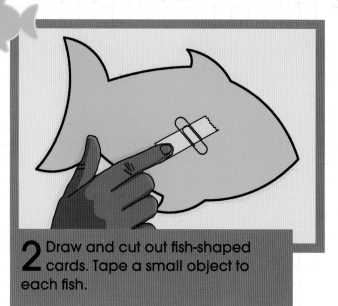

2 Draw and cut out fish-shaped cards. Tape a small object to each fish.

YOU WILL NEED:

- string
- wooden spoon
- strong magnet
- pencil
- card
- scissors
- sticky tape
- variety of small objects

3 Go fishing! Try to pick up each fish in turn with the magnet. Which objects stick to it best?

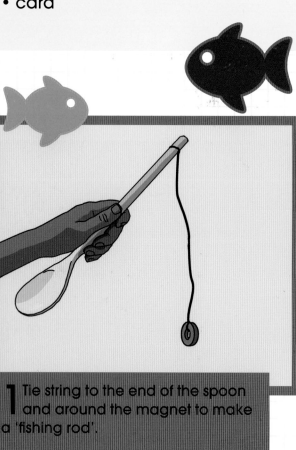

1 Tie string to the end of the spoon and around the magnet to make a 'fishing rod'.

Substances that contain iron, such as steel, are attracted to magnets. Paper clips, nails and washers should work well. Drawing pins and metal fasteners may work – but they could be made of other metals.

GLOSSARY

CONDUCTOR
A substance that carries electricity. Copper is a good electrical conductor.

ELECTROMAGNET
A device with an iron core surrounded by a coil of wire. When electricity passes through the coil, the core is magnetised.

FORCE
Action on an object that causes its motion to change speed or direction. Gravity and friction are types of force.

GALVANIZED
Coated with zinc.

GRAVITY
A force that attracts objects to each other.

GRID
A system for distributing electric power throughout a region.

INSULATOR
A substance that does not carry electricity.

OPAQUE
Describes a substance that does not let light pass through it. Wood is opaque.

PITCH
How high or low a sound is.

PRISM
A transparent object that breaks up light into the different colours of the rainbow.

TRANSPARENT
Describes a substance that does let light pass through it. Glass is transparent.

ULTRASOUND
Sounds with such a high frequency that humans cannot hear them.

VIBRATING
Moving to and fro or up and down very quickly and repeateadly.

VOLUME
How loud or quiet a sound is.

WAVELENGTH
The distance between one peak or trough of a sound or light wave to the next peak or trough.

INDEX

FURTHER INFORMATION

www.bbc.co.uk/schools/ks2bitesize/
science/physical_processes
Games and quizzes on physics.

www.sciencekids.co.nz/physics.html
Information, projects and games on
things to do with physics.